為什麼樹葉掉了

Sharing the Planet | Non-Fiction Series

Copyright © 2022 by Level Learning, INC. and Washington Yu Ying PCS™
Original and Edited Text Copyright © 2022 by Washington Yu Ying PCS™

All rights reserved. No part of this book in whole or part may be reproduced without written permission from the publisher.

Published by Level Learning, INC.

Content Contributors:
Washington Yu Ying PCS™ - Qianyi (Shirley) Zhang, Pearl Zao He You
Level Learning - Jingyao Qi

Illustrations by: Matt Austin, Josh Taira

Leveling classification based on Level Learning standard.
For full description, visit www.levellearning.com

ISBN 978-1-64040-067-2
Traditional Chinese Edition

About Level Learning:

Level Learning provides a literacy focused curriculum specifically designed for K-12 Chinese as a Second Language classrooms. Our program offers 20 levels of specific and detailed objectives, leveled texts and passages, mastery-based online assessment, and analytics to enable data-driven instruction. Level Learning reading curriculum for both literature and informational text emphasize grammar and comprehension skills to help teachers develop confident and independent Chinese language readers. The non-fiction series of books are specifically designed to support our informational text course based on multiple national standards. To learn more about our entire offering, visit www.levellearning.com.

About Washington Yu Ying PCS™:

Washington Yu Ying PCS is a Mandarin English dual language immersion International Baccalaureate (IB) World school. Yu Ying's mission is to inspire and prepare young people to create a better world by challenging them to reach their full potential in a nurturing Chinese/English educational environment. Yu Ying's comprehensive IB, dual immersion curriculum equips students with global competencies for success in the real world. As a leader in immersion education, Yu Ying is determined to advance Chinese language programs and global citizenry education by helping other schools create and strengthen their Chinese programs. For more information, email: products@washingtonyuying.org

樹木的生長離不開陽光、空氣和水。陽光、空氣和水是怎麼幫助樹木生長的呢?

和動物一樣，樹木也需要呼吸。樹根會吸收水，然後把水輸送到樹葉上。樹葉也會從空氣中吸收水分。

樹葉把水、陽光和空氣變成營養。

樹葉再把營養輸送給樹幹。樹木就是這樣生長的。

秋天到了。天氣開始變冷,陽光和水也開始變少。

沒有足夠的水和陽光，樹木需要的營養就不夠了。

樹木會死掉嗎?當然不會。樹木會在內部切斷和樹葉的聯繫。樹葉就會慢慢變黃、變乾。

沒多久，樹葉就掉下來了。

這樣，樹木可以生存下來。第二年春天，樹木會長出新的葉子。

Glossary

	Pinyin	English Definition
生長	shēng zhǎng	growth
離不開	lí bu kāi	inseparable
陽光	yáng guāng	sunshine
空氣	kōng qì	air
需要	xū yào	need
呼吸	hū xī	to breathe
輸送	shū sòng	to transport
樹葉	shù yè	leaf
變	biàn	to change
營養	yíng yǎng	nutrition
樹幹	shù gàn	tree trunk
秋天	qiū tiān	autumn
開始	kāi shǐ	start
冷	lěng	cold
少	shǎo	less

	Pinyin	English Definition
足夠	zú gòu	enough
不夠	bú gòu	not enough
內部	nèi bù	inside
切斷	qiē duàn	to cut off
聯繫	lián xì	link
乾	gān	dry
掉	diào	fall
生存	shēng cún	to survive

www.ingramcontent.com/pod-product-compliance
Lightning Source LLC
Chambersburg PA
CBHW041223070526
44584CB00001B/69